Contents

D1038736

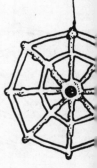

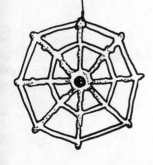

Creepy Cookies

By Tina Vilicich-Solomon

Illustrated by Dianne O'Quinn Burke

KidBacks™

RANDOM HOUSE 🏠 NEW YORK

EVERY RECIPE IN THIS BOOK SHOULD BE CARRIED OUT UNDER
ADULT SUPERVISION AT ALL TIMES

Library of Congress Cataloging-in-Publication Data
Vilicich-Solomon, Tina.
   Creepy cookies / by Tina Vilicich-Solomon ; illustrated by Dianne O'Quinn Burke.
    p. cm.
   Summary: A collection of recipes for making Halloween cookies with such names
as Bloody Bones, Cutoff Cats' Tails, and Toasted Tombstones. Includes basic baking
instructions and kitchen hints.
   ISBN 0-679-86957-3 (pbk.)
   http://www.randomhouse.com/
   1. Cookies—Juvenile literature. 2. Halloween cookery—Juvenile literature.
[1. Cookies. 2. Baking. 3. Halloween cookery.] I. Burke, Dianne O'Quinn. ill. II. Title.
TX772.V55 1996
641.8'654—dc20   95-47656

Printed in the United States of America

10 9 8 7 6 5 4 3 2 1

KIDBACKS is a trademark of Random House, Inc.

Introduction

Are you bored with the usual goody-goody cookies? Do you want to shake up—even shock—the oatmeal-raisin crowd? Well, then, plunge into the oodles of icky recipes in *Creepy Cookies,* because nothing satisfies faster than festering finger foods! Whether you're mixing dough for Fruity Phlegmballs or baking Brain Bundles, you can count on screams of horror when guests peek into your cookie jar. But don't worry, after they've tasted your ghastly goodies, they'll be screaming for more! Because the treats in *Creepy Cookies* taste every bit as yummy as the ones your dear sweet grandma used to bake.

Though you're anxious to start baking, don't foam at the mouth just yet. You'll need to read up on basic baking guidelines, because while your cookies should be scary, your time in the kitchen shouldn't!

Let's Get Started

1. **Always ask an adult to help you when the recipe calls for sharp utensils, appliances, the oven, or the stove.**

2. Always wash your hands thoroughly with soap and water before you begin handling food.

3. Turn saucepan handles to the side, so they don't get knocked off the stove. Also, make sure saucepan lids and covers are opened away from the face to avoid steam burns.

4. Use potholders or wear oven mitts when removing a pot or pan from the oven (or whenever you're handling any hot pot or pan).

5. Never leave anything cooking on the stovetop without supervision.

6. If you spill something on the floor, wipe it up quickly so no one will slip.

7. Clean as you go! You're sure to be welcomed back into the kitchen if you leave it as you found it. Hey, give 'em a real scare—leave it even cleaner!

8. Read through the recipe before you begin to bake, to make sure you have all the necessary ingredients, tools, and supplies.

9. If you've got long hair, be sure to tie it back so it won't get into the food.

10. Always have a fire extinguisher in your kitchen, and know how to use it!

Trouble Shooting

Here are some important tips to make your sweet concoctions as perfectly petrifying as possible!

On Mixing and Baking

- Always mix batter with ingredients at room temperature—especially eggs and butter (or margarine).

- Overmixing can toughen the texture of the cookie, so try not to over-beat cookie dough.

- For best results, bake cookies with the oven shelves in the center of the oven.

- When using an ovenproof glass pan, reduce the oven temperature by 25 degrees to prevent overbaking.

- Always start with a baking sheet at room temperature. Place cookies about 2 inches apart (unless otherwise indicated). Any closer and they could spread together when baking; any farther apart and they could burn.

On Handling and Storage

- Remember to clear a safe place to put the cookie sheet, and put potholders down before you pull cookies out of the oven.

- Use a metal spatula to lift cookies off cookie sheets.

- If you like cookies on the crisp side, do not close the cookie container tightly—a little circulating air will help keep them crunchy. For chewier textures, store cookies in an airtight container.

- Never store two types of cookies in one container. It makes both types less flavorful, and can change the cookies' texture.

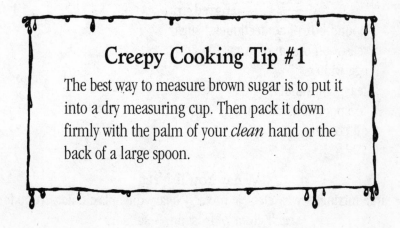

Creepy Cooking Tip #1

The best way to measure brown sugar is to put it into a dry measuring cup. Then pack it down firmly with the palm of your *clean* hand or the back of a large spoon.

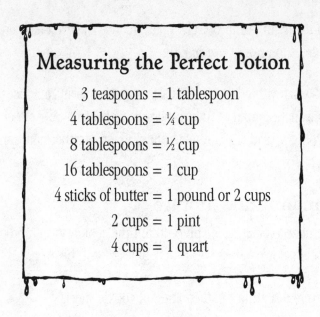

Measuring the Perfect Potion

3 teaspoons = 1 tablespoon

4 tablespoons = ¼ cup

8 tablespoons = ½ cup

16 tablespoons = 1 cup

4 sticks of butter = 1 pound or 2 cups

2 cups = 1 pint

4 cups = 1 quart

Frighteningly Good Frosting

There's no magic art to decorating cookies. The secret's in the frosting! Many of the recipes in this book call for frosting, either to use as a decorating technique or as an adhesive. You can make your own frosting using this recipe. Or you can buy ready-made *decorating* frosting in a tube.

Ingredients
1-pound box of confectioners' sugar
¾ teaspoon cream of tartar
3 egg whites
¼ teaspoon vanilla
¼ teaspoon almond extract
food coloring

What You'll Need
• large mixing bowl • electric mixer • heavy-duty plastic bags (one for each color of frosting) • scissors

Directions

1. Place all ingredients (except food coloring) in a large mixing bowl. Beat well until fluffy and well blended (this takes about 5 to 7 minutes).

2. Add food coloring as desired. If you want more than one color, divide the frosting into two bowls. Add the color one drop at a time until you create the desired shade.

3. Fill each heavy-duty plastic bag with a different color frosting. Snip off the corner of each bag with scissors. If you're using a pastry bag, follow instructions on package for fitting the pastry tips.

4. Before you begin decorating, slowly squirt out a small amount of frosting to eliminate air pockets. When you're done, place unused frosting in an airtight container. This will keep in the refrigerator for up to two months.

Makes: About 1½ cups

Creepy Cooking Tip #2

Before you allow stick margarine or butter to soften, cut the stick to the correct amount, using the measurement marks written on the wrapper as a guide. Then bring margarine or butter to room temperature.

CREEPED-OUT CUTOUTS

Cutout cookies are a "slice of (cookie) life" you and your friends won't want to miss! And they're easy to create. Some recipes call for the cookie dough to be cut, while other recipes have you cut already-baked cookies. For a perfectly wretched cookie presentation, follow these simple rules:

- Always allow already-baked cookies to cool completely before cutting. Once they're cool, lay your pattern over the top of one of the cookies. Always ask an adult to help you cut out your cookie shapes with a serrated knife. Use a gentle sawing motion to cut through each cookie.

- When patterns or cookie cutters are required, be sure to place the patterns as close together as possible.

- Some of the recipes call for the dough to be firm and chilled. Put the dough in the refrigerator until you need it. Most cutout cookie recipes require dough to chill for at least an hour. If time permits, chill dough overnight.

- When you are asked to roll out dough with a rolling pin, sprinkle flour on a smooth surface and over the rolling pin to prevent the dough from sticking.

Now look ahead to find a batch of *chilling* cutout cookie recipes that are definitely worth the wait!

Freaky Finger Food

These funky fingers are horribly good—hands down!

Ingredients

1 cup all-purpose flour
2 tablespoons cornstarch
⅛ teaspoon salt
½ cup unsalted butter, softened
½ cup confectioners' sugar, sifted
½ teaspoon vanilla
⅓ cup very finely chopped pecans
⅓ cup medium-coarse chopped pecans
¼ cup sliced almonds

What You'll Need

• flour sifter • small mixing bowl • kitchen fork • large mixing bowl
• electric mixer • waxed paper • rolling pin • ruler • butter knife
• metal spatula • baking sheet • potholders • wire rack

Directions

1. Ask an adult to help you preheat the oven to 300°. Sift the flour and place it in a small mixing bowl. Add the cornstarch and salt. Stir together with a fork and set aside.

2. Place butter in a large mixing bowl and cream with an electric mixer. Sift in the sugar. Mix together until batter is fluffy. Add vanilla and pecans and blend well. Now slowly pour the flour mixture into the butter mixture, and combine until dough appears crumbly.

3. Place a
piece of waxed
paper about 12
inches long onto
a smooth work
surface. Place the
dough on top of
the waxed paper,
then cover it with
another piece of

waxed paper about the same size. With a rolling pin, roll out the dough
to ¼ inch thick and slowly remove the top piece of paper.

4. Slice the dough with a butter knife into oblong shapes about the
width of your middle finger. Use a metal spatula to lift the fingers onto
an ungreased cookie sheet, making sure you leave about 1 inch in
between each finger.

5. To give fingers an old and knotted appearance, bend some of them
sideways at the knuckles. Use slivered almonds for each fingernail.

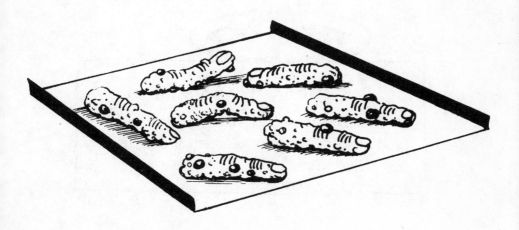

6. With an adult's help, place baking sheet in the oven for 12 to 15 minutes. Then remove with potholders and transfer the cookies with the metal spatula to wire rack to cool.

Makes: About 18 decrepit digits

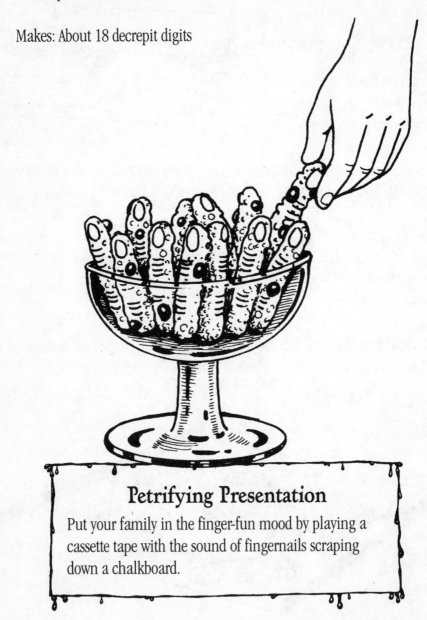

Petrifying Presentation

Put your family in the finger-fun mood by playing a cassette tape with the sound of fingernails scraping down a chalkboard.

Fetid Athlete's Feet

These foul feet leave a trail of flakes wherever they fester!

Ingredients

2 cups sifted flour
1 teaspoon baking powder
1 teaspoon salt
1 cup butter
½ cup granulated sugar
½ cup brown sugar
2 eggs
1 tablespoon milk

1 teaspoon vanilla
1 cup (6 ounces) butter-
   scotch chips
1 small tube of yellow
   ready-made frosting
30 raisins
½ cup confectioners' sugar

What You'll Need

• waxed paper • pencil • scissors • ruler • 13- by 9-inch baking pan
• small mixing bowl • kitchen fork • large mixing bowl
• electric mixer • rubber spatula • potholders • wire rack
• serrated knife • metal spatula • chopping block or cutting board

Directions

1. Preheat oven to 350°. Take a piece of waxed paper 3 by 5 inches and draw the outline of a foot. (You can draw a left or right foot outline, or even make two patterns for both feet.) Cut it out and set it aside.

2. Take another piece of waxed paper, 13 by 17 inches. Make a 3-inch cut from each corner in toward the center. (The cuts help to prevent paper from bunching up in the corners of the pan.) Now lay the paper on the bottom of the baking pan and fold up sides so they extend upward beyond the rim.

15

3. Place flour, baking powder, and salt in a small mixing bowl. Stir with a fork and set aside. With an adult's help, use an electric mixer to cream the butter and sugars together in a large mixing bowl. Then add eggs, milk, vanilla, flour mixture, and butterscotch chips, mixing well after each ingredient. Continue to beat.

4. Scoop dough into prepared pan, using a rubber spatula to spread the dough evenly.

5. Place the pan in the oven and bake for 25 to 30 minutes until the top is lightly browned. Carefully remove the pan with potholders and place on a wire rack to cool. For now, you will have one solid cookie.

6. When the pan is completely cooled, ask an adult to help you remove the cookie. Using a serrated knife, cut the cookie into six equal bars. Then slide a metal spatula under each bar, lift away from the paper, and place on a chopping block or cutting board.

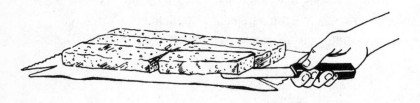

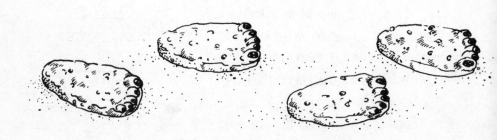

7. Lay your footprint pattern on top of a bar and cut out the footprint shape. Do this for each bar until you have six cookie feet in front of you. Squirt a dot of yellow frosting on each toe and stick one raisin on top of each bit of frosting.

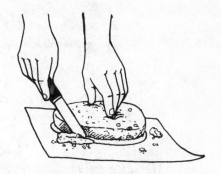

8. Sprinkle confectioners' sugar on a piece of waxed paper, and set the bottom side of each infected foot in it.

Makes: 6 foul footsies

Petrifying Presentation

Gross out your company by serving foot cream on the side. Peel the label off a bottle of foot cream and glue it to a container of caramel sauce. Then invite your guests to drizzle it over the top of the craggy toes.

Or wrap up a dozen Fetid Athlete's Feet in a shoebox, tie it up with an old shoelace, and give the package to your favorite stinky-footed pal.

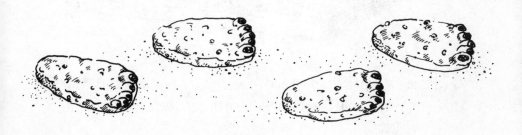

Mucous Munchies

These postnasal drip cookies are nothing to sneeze at!

Ingredients

16-ounce roll of ready-made oatmeal chocolate chip cookie dough
6-ounce box of tapioca pudding, along with the ingredients listed
  on package
1 envelope of unflavored gelatin
1 cup nondairy whipped topping

What You'll Need

• utility knife • ruler • greased and floured 13- by 9- by 2-inch pan
• potholders • medium saucepan • whisk • rubber spatula

Directions

1. Ask an adult to help you preheat the oven to 325°. Carefully cut
dough roll into ¼-inch-thick disks with a utility knife, and lay them
flat on the bottom of the prepared pan. When the dough bakes, it will
spread out, covering most of the pan.

2. Place the pan in the oven and bake for 20 to 25 minutes. Then
remove from oven with the potholders and set on a heat-safe surface to
cool completely.

18

3. With an adult's help, prepare tapioca pudding in the saucepan as indicated on the package. Turn off burner and use your whisk to stir in the envelope of unflavored gelatin. When saucepan is cool enough, place it in the refrigerator for 30 minutes (this will partially set the tapioca mixture).

4. When the tapioca is nearly set, it will have a shiny, "just coughed up" texture! Fold in the whipped topping with a rubber spatula, then spread the mixture onto the cooled cookie bars.

5. With an adult's help, use the utility knife to cut the pan of cookies into individual bars, and return pan to refrigerator to set tapioca completely. To store, wrap Mucous Munchies in plastic wrap and put in the refrigerator.

Serves: 24 heavy hackers

Petrifying Presentation

Serve each Mucous Munchie on a facial tissue instead of a napkin. That way, your friends and family will be ready should they get the urge to cough up at the table!

Toasted Tombstones

May you rest in peace—with one of these yummy cookies under your belt.

Ingredients

1¼ cups cake flour
¼ teaspoon baking soda
¼ teaspoon salt
½ cup unsalted butter (not margarine), softened
¼ cup confectioners' sugar
¼ cup sour cream
¼ cup finely chopped almonds
decorating frosting (see recipe on page 8) or ready-made
    frosting in white or black

What You'll Need

• small mixing bowl • kitchen fork • large mixing bowl
• electric mixer • ruler • chopping knife • cookie sheets
• potholders • metal spatula • wire rack

Directions

1. Preheat oven to 350°. Place flour, baking soda, and salt in a small mixing bowl. Stir with a fork and set aside.

2. Put butter and confectioners' sugar together in a large bowl. Then ask an adult to help you cream them together with an electric mixer. Add sour cream, then stir in flour mixture and almonds. Blend well until smooth.

3. Scoop out dough onto a smooth, lightly floured work surface. Pat into a rectangle ¾ inch thick and 5 inches wide. Cut the rectangle into twelve bars with a chopping knife. Each bar should be approximately 1½ inches wide by 2½ inches long.

4. Arrange cookie bars about 1 inch apart on ungreased cookie sheets. With an adult's help, place them in the oven and bake for 8 to 10 minutes. Cookies will puff slightly and expand during baking. Remove cookie sheets from the oven with potholders and immediately transfer cookies with a metal spatula to a wire rack to cool.

5. When tombstones are completely cooled, decorate each one with a friend's name and today's date or simply write "R.I.P" (Rest in Peace) and add on a few frosting flowers.

Makes: Approximately 12 gruesome tombstones

Petrifying Presentation

These cookies look especially ghastly when served with ice cream—just stick one into each rounded scoop. Try flavors that will look like a fresh dirt mound, such as Rocky Road.

Lipsmacking Lunatics

You'll go crazy over these insanely delicious cookies!

Ingredients

3¼ cups all-purpose flour
½ teaspoon baking soda
¼ teaspoon salt
1 teaspoon ground cinnamon
2 teaspoons ground ginger
¼ teaspoon ground nutmeg
¼ teaspoon ground cloves
1 cup butter or margarine, softened
¾ cup dark brown sugar, firmly packed
1 large egg

½ cup unsulfurized molasses
chow mein noodles
round, flat white-chocolate wafer candies (such as Wilton Microwave Candy Melts, available at craft and baking supply stores)
16 to 18 tiny red cinnamon candies
small tube of ready-made frosting, blue

What You'll Need

• kitchen fork • medium bowl • large bowl • electric mixer
• plastic wrap • rolling pin • ruler
• 4-inch round plastic lid (coffee can lids or margarine tub lids are ideal) • knife • 1-inch round plastic bottle top (bottled-water caps work well) • greased cookie sheet
• potholders • metal spatula

Directions

1. Stir together flour, baking soda, salt, cinnamon, ginger, nutmeg, and cloves in a medium bowl. Then set the mixture aside.

2. With an adult's help, cream butter and sugar together in a large bowl with an electric mixer. Add egg, molasses, and the flour mixture and continue to beat until the mixture is smooth (don't overmix).

3. Divide dough into two equal parts, then wrap each half with plastic wrap. Place in the refrigerator and chill for about two hours (or until firm). Preheat oven to 325°.

4. Unwrap one of the dough balls, place it on a floured surface, and roll until ¼ inch thick. Use your coffee can lid to cut out circles as close together as possible. Then use the bottle cap to cut out a wide-open mouth in the lower portion of each cookie. Remove the mouth cutout and carefully lay each lunatic on a greased cookie sheet, about 3 inches apart.

5. Insert chow mein noodles for hair, and use two wafers for eyes. Wedge one cinnamon candy into the top of the "mouth" as an uvula (also known as the dangly thing that hangs down the back of a screaming person's throat).

6. Repeat with second ball of dough. Then have an adult help you place the cookie sheet in the oven for 9 to 11 minutes. Remove from the oven and transfer to a cool, flat surface. After cookies are completely cool, squirt dots of blue frosting into the center of each white-chocolate wafer for eyeballs.

Serves: Multiple personalities (but they'll all have to share 18 cookies)

Petrifying Presentation

Turn your lunatic into a slobbering idiot: serve up some drool on the side for dipping. Stir together 1 cup confectioners' sugar and ¾ cup milk (add more milk if you prefer more runny drool).

Cutoff Cats' Tails

Sink your fangs into this purrrrfectly disgusting dessert.

Ingredients

2½ cups all-purpose flour, sifted
1 teaspoon baking soda
1 teaspoon cream of tartar
½ teaspoon salt
1 cup butter or margarine, softened
1½ cups (plus 3 tablespoons) confectioners' sugar
1 egg, beaten
1 teaspoon vanilla extract
½ teaspoon almond extract
⅛ cup confectioners' sugar
2 tablespoons unsweetened cocoa powder
1 tablespoon cinnamon
⅛ cup granulated sugar
strawberry jelly

What You'll Need

• flour sifter • small mixing bowl • large mixing bowl
• plastic wrap • ungreased cookie sheet • kitchen fork
• potholders • small rubber spatula • small bowl

Directions

1. Combine sifted flour, baking soda, cream of tartar, and salt into a small bowl. Stir together and set aside.

2. Place butter and 1½ cups of confectioners' sugar in a large mixing bowl and beat thoroughly until creamy (remember, always ask an adult

25

to help you with this). Add egg and extracts, then flour mixture, and continue beating until dough is smooth. Remove from bowl, cover in plastic wrap, and chill in the refrigerator for at least an hour. Preheat the oven to 350°.

3. Sprinkle a teaspoon of confectioners' sugar into the palms of your hands. Scoop out 2 tablespoons of cookie dough and rub it back and forth until it's the size and shape of a hot dog. One end should be slightly more tapered than the other. Place on an ungreased cookie sheet and repeat with the remaining dough.

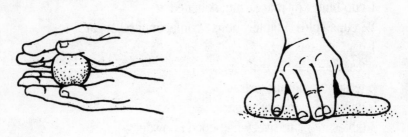

4. Using a kitchen fork, gently rake in short, lengthwise strokes all the way down the tail. Then bend the tip upward (we want it to look real, after all!).

5. With an adult's help, put the cats' tails in the oven for 15 to 17 minutes. Transfer cookie sheet with potholders to a flat surface to completely cool.

6. Decorate tails so that they appear to have been ripped off from a variety of cats. For white cats: Place the 3 tablespoons of *confectioners'* sugar into flour sifter and sprinkle over tail. For brown cats: Place cocoa powder into sifter and sprinkle. For calico cats: Mix *granulated* sugar with cinnamon in a small bowl, then sprinkle. Use a rubber spatula to dab a spot of jelly onto the base of each cat's tail where it was once attached!

Makes: About 15 tasty tails

Petrifying Presentation

Turn into a tail-less cat by drawing whiskers on your face and pinning pointed cardboard ears on your head. As you serve the tails to your pals, howl in anguish.

Burnt Bat Wings

Here's a macabre munchie to serve your batty buddies.

Ingredients
2 ready-made frozen pie crusts, thawed and chilled
4 to 5 ¾-ounce large grape-flavored fruit rolls
   (such as Sunkist Real Fruit Snack Fruit Roll-Ups)
ultra-thin black licorice whips
¼ cup granulated sugar

What You'll Need
• pencil • waxed paper • ruler • scissors • cutting board
• utility knife • ungreased baking sheet • rubber spatula
• potholders • wire rack • metal spatula

Directions

1. With an adult's help, preheat the oven to 350°.

2. Sketch out a bat wing pattern about 3
inches long on a piece of waxed paper. (Bats'
wings are arched on top with three scallops
on the bottom. You may want to use a lid to
make your rounded scallops even.) Use scissors to cut out your pattern and set it aside.

3. Remove wrapping and lining from thawed pie crust and lay it flat
onto a floured cutting board. Lay the bat wing pattern on the edge of the
crust. Ask an adult to help you trim around the pattern with a utility knife.
Repeat with remaining crust, then put all the wings onto a baking sheet.

4. Lay a fruit roll on the cutting board and put the bat wing pattern on top. Carefully cut out the bat wing pattern and set aside.

5. Next, lay the strip of licorice over the bat's wing. Measure from the center of the wing (where it attaches to the body) to each of the three scalloped points, making sure the licorice is slightly curved. Ask an adult to help you cut the licorice, and set aside (you should have a short, medium, and long piece of licorice for each bat's wing).

6. Sprinkle sugar evenly over each bat's wing. Arch the licorice pieces slightly, and lay each piece on top of the cookie. Place a fruit roll cutout directly on top. Repeat with the other wings.

7. Place baking sheet in the oven for 15 to 17 minutes. Fruit rolls will soften and melt slightly. Using potholders, remove cookie sheet from the oven, and allow it to cool on a wire rack. When cool, remove wings from the cookie sheet with a metal spatula.

Makes: 10 to 12
wicked wings

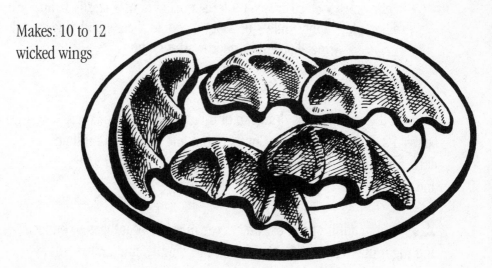

29

Bloody Bones

Need to satisfy your craving for blood?
Then suck the life out of these sugary sweets!

Ingredients

2 cups all-purpose flour
½ teaspoon cardamom
¼ teaspoon salt
¾ cup butter
¾ cup granulated sugar
1 large egg, beaten
1 teaspoon vanilla extract
1 teaspoon thinly grated lemon peel
¼ cup red jelly (not jam)
¼ cup light corn syrup

What You'll Need

• waxed paper • pencil • ruler • scissors • medium mixing bowl
• kitchen fork • electric mixer • large mixing bowl • plastic wrap
• rolling pin • utility knife • ungreased cookie sheet • potholders
• metal spatula • microwave-safe bowl

Directions

1. On the waxed paper, draw two or three different-sized bones between 2 and 4 inches long. Cut them out and set aside. Combine flour, cardamom, and salt in a medium bowl, stir together with a fork, and set aside.

2. With an adult's help, use an electric mixer to beat together butter and sugar in a large mixing bowl. Add egg, vanilla, and grated lemon peel, and then gradually add the flour mixture. Beat until the ingredients are just combined—don't overmix. Remove dough from the bowl, wrap tightly in plastic, and chill in the refrigerator for at least an hour.

3. Preheat the oven to 325°. Divide the dough in two parts, then cover and return half to the refrigerator. Rub flour on a rolling pin and roll the remaining dough to a ¼-inch thickness on a smooth, floured surface. With your bone patterns, create "human" bones, using the knife and an adult's help. Repeat with the remaining dough ball, then place all the bones on an ungreased cookie sheet.

4. Place the cookie sheet in the oven and bake 13 to 15 minutes, or until slightly golden. Remove cookie sheet from the oven with potholders and let it cool. Once the cookies have cooled, remove the bones from the cookie sheet with a metal spatula.

5. Combine jelly and corn syrup in a microwave-safe serving bowl, and cover lightly with plastic wrap. Place the bowl in the microwave, and heat on high for 15 seconds. Repeat until the "blood" is warm and liquid (about 30 to 40 seconds). Carefully remove the bowl from the microwave with potholders, and pour immediately over the bones (blood can be covered in plastic wrap and stored in the refrigerator for up to one week).

Makes: 3 dozen cannibal crackers

Oozing Coffins

These crunchy coffins are a delicacy among the deceased.

Ingredients

¼ cup unsweetened cocoa powder
2 tablespoons cornstarch
1 cup all-purpose flour
¾ cup salted butter, softened
¾ cup confectioners' sugar
2 teaspoons vanilla extract
1 can ready-made chocolate cake frosting
1 cup red raspberry jam

What You'll Need

• small mixing bowl • kitchen fork • large mixing bowl
• electric mixer • plastic wrap • rolling pin • ruler
• utility knife • baking sheet • potholders
• small rubber spatula • spoon • metal spatula

Directions

1. Place cocoa, cornstarch, and flour together in a small mixing bowl, stir with a fork, and set aside.

2. With an adult's help, cream together butter and sugar with an electric mixer in a large mixing bowl. Add in vanilla and the flour mixture and blend thoroughly. Roll dough into a ball, wrap tightly in plastic wrap, and place in the refrigerator for at least 1½ hours.

3. Preheat the oven to 325°. Break the dough in two, then rewrap one half and return it to the refrigerator. Roll out the other half of the dough to ¼-inch thickness, using a well-floured rolling pin. Cut 2-inch by 1-inch rectangles, then snip off the corners on one end. Repeat with the remaining dough ball. Then place all the coffins on a baking sheet.

4. Ask an adult to help you place the coffins into the oven. Bake for 16 to 18 minutes, then, using potholders, transfer the cookies to a cool, flat surface.

5. When the cookies have completely cooled, spread ready-made chocolate frosting on half of the cookies with a small rubber spatula. Use a spoon to top each of these with raspberry jam, but do not spread around. Gently place a second plain cookie on top of each frosted half and press lightly. Just watch as the rotting carcass comes oozing out!

Makes: About 18 deadly beds

Petrifying Presentation

Oh, no! The mortician has forgotten the formaldehyde! Serve your guests clear uncola soda instead to help them decompose their sweet treat.

Also, you can easily vary this recipe using a wide range of icky oozes in your coffins, depending on your taste. A "clean-colored" ooze could be a mixture of confectioners' sugar and milk. Or cut out simple cadaver shapes from fruit rolls for flat, crusty insides. Or for a sticky, gooey, and oh-so-yummy ooze, try peanut butter and marshmallow creme.

HORRIFYING HAND-SHAPED COOKIES

Your own hands can make the creepiest-looking cookies in the kitchen! Just a couple of things to keep in mind while baking hand-shaped treats:

- Always wash your hands before digging into the cookie dough.

- The thinner you make the cookie, the more likely it is that it will break.

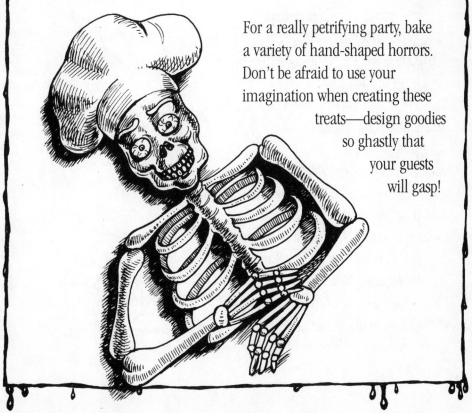

For a really petrifying party, bake a variety of hand-shaped horrors. Don't be afraid to use your imagination when creating these treats—design goodies so ghastly that your guests will gasp!

Decomposed Digits

Hunks of human flesh are the secret to these finger-lickin'-good cookies.

Ingredients
red and clear gumdrops (about a dozen of each)
16-ounce roll of ready-made sugar cookie dough
1½ ounces dry green gelatin

What You'll Need
• utility knife • rolling pin • plastic wrap • ruler •
• ungreased baking sheet • metal spatula • wire rack

Directions
1. With an adult's help, preheat oven to 350°. Then ask the adult to help you cut the gumdrops lengthwise, from top to base. Set aside. These will be the nail tips.

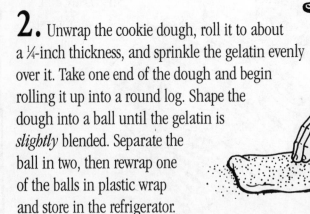

2. Unwrap the cookie dough, roll it to about a ¼-inch thickness, and sprinkle the gelatin evenly over it. Take one end of the dough and begin rolling it up into a round log. Shape the dough into a ball until the gelatin is *slightly* blended. Separate the ball in two, then rewrap one of the balls in plastic wrap and store in the refrigerator.

3. Gently mold the other piece of dough into finger and toe shapes about ¼ inch thick. Place the shapes on an ungreased baking sheet about 1½ inches apart, and set a nail tip on each body part.

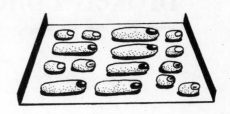

4. Place the baking sheet in the oven for 7 to 11 minutes, or until the cookies are slightly golden. Remove and transfer to wire racks to cool. When the cookies are cool, use a metal spatula to remove from the cookie sheet.

Makes: About 4 dozen nose pickers and tire kickers

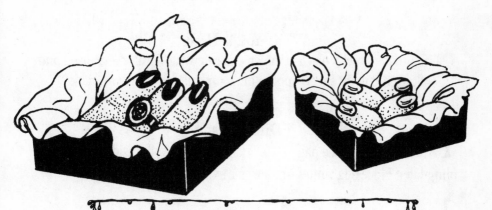

Petrifying Presentation

Pick up plastic jewelry at a local store and slip rings on your gangrenous fingers. Then stick the decorated digits in a gift box. Nothing freaks out a friend more than opening a small package, only to find a few severed fingers and toes. . . . So what are you waiting for?

Broken Bone Crunchers

Nothing beats the snap of just-broken bones.

Ingredients

4 eggs
1¼ cups granulated sugar
½ teaspoon baking powder
½ teaspoon almond extract
1½ cups sliced almonds
1¾ cups all-purpose flour
¼ cup crystallized sugar (large granulated)

What You'll Need

• large mixing bowl • electric mixer • plastic wrap • ruler • greased and floured baking sheet • potholders • metal spatula • wire rack

Directions

1. Separate eggs (see page 78 for help) and put yolks aside for scrambling later. Place egg whites in a large mixing bowl.

2. Add granulated sugar, baking powder, and almond extract. With an adult's help, use an electric mixer to thoroughly blend the ingredients. Add almonds, flour, and finally, crystallized sugar. Continue to beat on slow speed until well mixed. Remove from the bowl, cover tightly in plastic wrap, and chill in the refrigerator for one hour. Preheat the oven to 325°.

3. Take 3 tablespoons of dough, roll it into a tube shape (about 3 inches long), and place on a greased and floured baking sheet. Repeat with the remaining dough.

4. Put the cookie sheet in the oven for 15 to 20 minutes until the cookies are light golden. Remove from the oven with potholders and allow to cool until the cookies are slightly warm to the touch.

5. The cookies have expanded, so to mold bones into shape, take the cookie between your hands and roll it carefully to form a hot-dog-shaped tube. Gently squeeze the cookie together in the palm of your hands so that the cookie sticks out slightly on each side (near your thumb on one end and your pinky finger on the other). Form the ends of the bones by pinching cookie ends out into a heart shape.

Makes: 24 fancy femurs

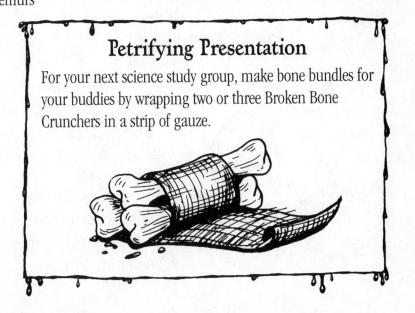

Petrifying Presentation

For your next science study group, make bone bundles for your buddies by wrapping two or three Broken Bone Crunchers in a strip of gauze.

Bloodshot Eyeballs

Watch these eyeballs disappear in a wink!

Ingredients

2½ cups flour
½ teaspoon salt
black licorice vines
   (very thin licorice,
   less than ⅛ inch thick)
20 raisins
3 rolls of lime-flavor Life
   Savers or other similar
   round, hard candy

¼ cup butter
1 cup granulated sugar
½ teaspoon baking soda
½ cup sour cream
1 egg
½ tablespoon grated
   lemon rind
½ teaspoon vanilla
ready-made frosting, red

What You'll Need

• small mixing bowl • kitchen fork • utility knife • ruler
• electric mixer • large mixing bowl • plastic wrap
• ungreased baking sheet • potholders • wire rack
• toothpick • metal spatula

Directions

1. Place flour and salt in a small mixing bowl and stir together with a fork. Set aside. Use your utility knife to cut six slices of black licorice vine for each eye as eyelashes, making each ¼ to ½ inch long. Set aside.

Press a raisin into the center hole of each Life Saver and set aside.

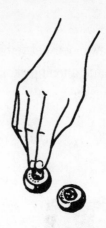

2. With an adult's help, use an electric mixer to cream the butter and sugar together in a large mixing bowl until fluffy and smooth. Add baking soda, sour cream, egg, grated lemon rind, and vanilla, and blend well. Gradually stir in the flour mixture.

3. Separate the dough into two balls and wrap each in plastic wrap. Refrigerate at least 1½ hours.

4. Preheat oven to 375°. Take one of the balls of dough from the refrigerator and roll several small smooth balls, putting them onto an ungreased baking sheet. Gently pinch opposite ends of each cookie to form a human eye shape.

5. Put one Life Saver in the center of each eye. Press eyelashes into the top of each cookie. Continue with the remaining dough.

6. Place baking sheet into the oven for 10 to 12 minutes. Remove with potholders and allow to cool on a wire rack.

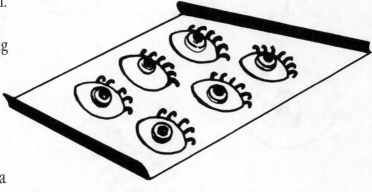

7. Draw bloodshot veins running through the eyes with ready-made frosting and a toothpick. Remove cookies from baking sheet with a metal spatula.

Makes: 20 psycho cyclopses

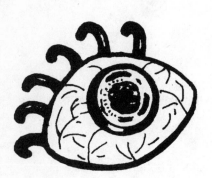

Petrifying Presentation

At your next sleepover, stick pairs of these eyeballs all over the house for your guests to stumble upon. They'll feel as if they're being watched all night!

Twisted Intestines

For a gut-wrenching good time, bake a batch of these shiny pink innards!

Ingredients

2 cups flour
½ teaspoon baking powder
6 tablespoons unsweetened
  cocoa
¼ teaspoon salt
¾ cup butter, softened
¾ cup granulated sugar

1 egg
2½ teaspoons vanilla
3 tablespoons milk
3 cups confectioners' sugar
2 tablespoons grenadine
  syrup
2 teaspoons vanilla

What You'll Need

• 2 small mixing bowls • large mixing bowl • electric mixer
• plastic wrap • ruler • ungreased baking sheet
• potholders • wire racks • metal spatula
• microwave-safe cup • 1-inch-wide pastry brush
or small rubber spatula

Directions

1. Stir flour, baking powder, cocoa, and salt together in a small mixing bowl, and set aside. With an adult's help, cream butter and granulated sugar together in a large mixing bowl with an electric mixer. In a separate bowl, beat together an egg and vanilla. Add egg mixture to creamed ingredients and blend well. Mix in flour mixture.

2. Divide the dough in half. Wrap each half tightly with plastic wrap and refrigerate for 3 hours.

43

3. Preheat the oven to 325°. Take 2 tablespoons of dough and roll the piece in your hands until it's about 6 inches long. Gently twist and put on an ungreased cookie sheet. Repeat until you have covered the sheet with small mounds of intestines. Each intestine pile should be about 3 inches wide, and about 2 inches apart from each other.

4. Place baking sheet in oven for 13 to 15 minutes. Using potholders, remove from oven and allow intestines to cool 2 to 3 minutes on wire racks. Transfer to a plate with a metal spatula.

5. To prepare frosting, pour milk in a microwave-safe cup and cover lightly with plastic wrap. Place cup in microwave and heat on high for 15 seconds (take care when you touch the plastic—steam is *very* hot!). Combine milk, confectioners' sugar, syrup, and vanilla in a small mixing bowl and stir until smooth. Frost intestines with rubber spatula or a 1-inch pastry brush. If frosting is too thick or too hard to spread, add one tablespoon milk and return to the microwave for 15 seconds, then restir.

Makes: About 4 dozen
gastro-intestinal
delights

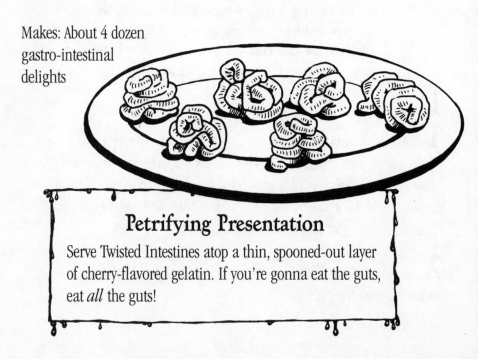

Petrifying Presentation

Serve Twisted Intestines atop a thin, spooned-out layer of cherry-flavored gelatin. If you're gonna eat the guts, eat *all* the guts!

Pus Poppers

Fresh pus simply oozes out in this dermatologist's delight.

Ingredients

2 dozen 2-inch round chocolate-fudge cookies
   (plain, no filling in middle)
1 large jar marshmallow creme
2 tablespoons milk
1 tablespoon water
½ teaspoon vanilla
1 tablespoon butter
1 square (1 ounce) unsweetened chocolate
1 cup confectioners' sugar

What You'll Need

• baking sheet • waxed paper • small mixing bowl
• microwave-safe bowl • potholders

Directions

1. Line cookie sheet with waxed paper and set aside.

2. To make one pus popper, turn a cookie bottom-side-up and place a teaspoon of marshmallow in center. Cover with a second cookie. Repeat with remaining cookies. Place on baking sheet and refrigerate for 20 minutes.

3. To make glaze, stir together milk, water, and vanilla in a small mixing bowl and set aside. In the microwave, melt butter and chocolate in a microwave-safe bowl on high for 2 minutes. Remove from the microwave with potholders and stir.

4. Stir in ⅓ cup of sugar. Add milk mixture and remaining confectioners' sugar, and stir well. Return the bowl to the microwave and heat until glaze is warm to the touch (the glaze should now be as thick as catsup).

5. To seal in the pus, roll entire edge of one cookie sandwich in the *warm* chocolate glaze. The glaze will harden quickly, sealing in your sickening surprise! Repeat with remaining cookies, then return baking sheet to the refrigerator to chill.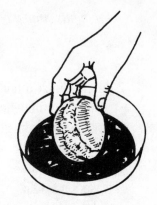

Makes: 12 gigantic pustules and pimples

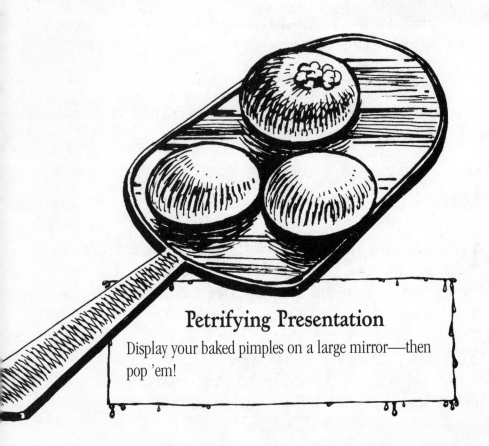

Petrifying Presentation
Display your baked pimples on a large mirror—then pop 'em!

Shrunken Heads

Don't lose your head over this gruesome goodie.

Ingredients

1½ cups all-purpose flour
1 teaspoon baking soda
½ teaspoon baking powder
¼ teaspoon salt
½ cup unsalted butter, softened
¾ cup chunky-style peanut butter
½ cup light brown sugar, packed
½ cup granulated sugar

2 eggs
3 tablespoons milk
2 teaspoons vanilla
8 1-inch round, white-chocolate wafers
½ cup coconut
food coloring, red and yellow
decorating frosting (see recipe on page 8) or ready-made frosting, red, blue, pink, and green

What You'll Need

• small mixing bowl • kitchen fork • electric mixer
• rubber spatula • large mixing bowl • greased and floured baking sheet
• potholders • wire rack

Directions

1. Preheat oven to 350°. Place flour, baking soda, baking powder, and salt in small mixing bowl, and stir together with a fork. Set aside.

2. With an adult's help, use an electric mixer to cream butter and peanut butter in a large mixing bowl. Beat in the sugars and eggs, then add milk and vanilla. Stirring continually with a rubber spatula, gradually add in flour mixture.

3. Divide the dough into twelve equal-size balls. Flatten each ball and spread them out evenly on the greased and floured baking sheet. Press two white-chocolate wafers into each head (these will be the eyes).

4. Bake the cookies in oven for 16 to 18 minutes. Using potholders, remove and allow heads to cool on a wire rack.

5. After all the heads have baked and cooled, you're ready to decorate. Place coconut in a small mixing bowl and stir in red and yellow food coloring. Add more food coloring until you get the shade of "carrot-top red" you want. Spread red frosting on the forehead (where hair will go), then press on about 1 tablespoon of colored-coconut hair.

6. To create ears, draw a capital G on the left (as you face it) and a backward capital G on the right, in pink frosting. Create eyeballs by squirting blue frosting onto the white-chocolate wafers. To create a snot-filled nose, squirt green frosting liberally into dots where nostrils would be. Draw on a pink mouth.

7. Finish the head off by squirting lots of red frosting around the neck. Ouch! Slide the heads onto a large serving platter.

Makes: 12 dead acne-prone shrunken redheads

48

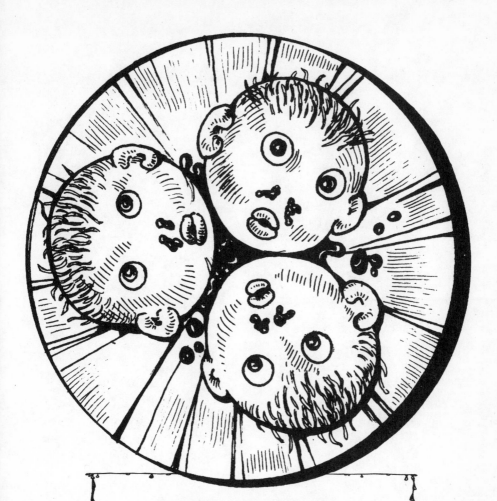

Petrifying Presentation

For your next spooky sleepover, bake several
Shrunken Heads, one for each guest. Then
have each friend decorate his or her own
decapitated head. Give an award for the most
dreadful creation.

MONSTER COOKIES

If it's got to be big and it's got to be bad, then you've got to whip up one of these monster-sized-cookie recipes. Here are a few handy hints to help make your baked beasties turn out perfect every time.

- With an adult's help, check "doneness" by inserting a toothpick into the center of the cookie. If it comes out clean, then it's ready!

- To prevent dryness, cool cookie completely on the sheet before cutting (unless otherwise indicated).

- Giant cookies break easily, so give your cookie support by lining the cookie sheet with foil before you begin. After cookie has baked and cooled, use the foil edges to slide it onto a large plate.

- Giant-sized cookies should be wrapped individually in plastic wrap.

These humongous cookies are designed to satisfy all your friends and family, or one *very hungry* monster.

Tarantula Treats

These warm, hairy spiders are guaranteed to creep
their way into your heart.

Ingredients

1½ cups all-purpose flour
⅓ cup cocoa powder (not hot chocolate mix)
½ cup butter, softened
¾ cup granulated sugar
1 teaspoon vanilla extract
1 large egg
10 cinnamon candies or mini red jelly beans
16-ounce can ready-made chocolate cake frosting
chocolate decorating sprinkles

What You'll Need

• small mixing bowl • kitchen fork • large mixing bowl
• electric mixer • plastic wrap • ungreased baking sheet
• potholders • small rubber spatula • 2 metal spatulas • serving plate

Directions

1. Place flour and cocoa in a small mixing bowl and mix together with a fork. Set aside.

2. With an adult's help, use an electric mixer to cream together butter and sugar in a large mixing bowl. Add vanilla, egg, and flour mixture. Blend until thoroughly mixed, then gather dough in a ball and wrap it in plastic wrap. Chill in the refrigerator for an hour. Preheat oven to 325°.

3. To make a tarantula, scoop out 1⅓ cups dough (return the rest to the refrigerator to keep it cold). Roll dough into nine logs about the thickness of your finger (eight of these will be legs). The two back legs should be the longest, followed by the four middle legs, and finally, the two front legs.

4. Take the ninth log, which should be about the length of one of the front legs, and bring the two ends together to create a circle. Place circle shape—the spider's body—on an ungreased baking sheet. Take the two longest logs and place them toward the back of its body. Press one end of each log into the open hole in the circle of dough.

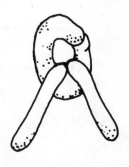

5. Place the middle-sized logs in the center of the hole, and the shortest legs toward the front of its body in the same manner as above. (As the legs are attached, the hole will fill in with dough.)

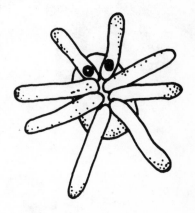

6. Poke two red candies (or mini jelly beans) close together at one end of its body as eyes. Continue making spiders with remaining dough.

7. Place baking sheet in oven for 15 to 20 minutes. Using potholders, remove from oven and cool tarantulas for 5 minutes.

8. Coat each tarantula with a thin layer of frosting, using a small rubber spatula, then sprinkle liberally with chocolate sprinkles. Transfer the tarantulas onto a serving plate using two metal spatulas.

Makes: 4 to 5 supersize spiders

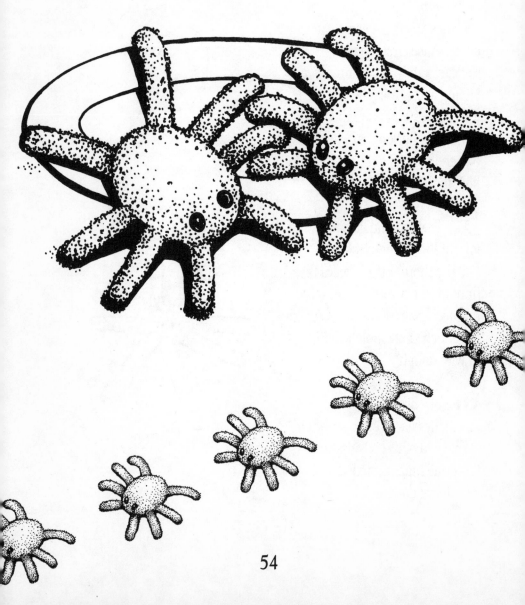

S-S-S-Squeezing Snake Snack

These s-s-s-supersize cookies are a great way to put the "squeeze" on latecomers!

Ingredients

8 tablespoons margarine or butter
1 cup oats
½ cup firmly packed brown sugar
½ cup flour
½ cup finely chopped walnuts
¼ teaspoon baking soda
1 can sweetened condensed milk
1 teaspoon vanilla extract
1 cup semisweet chocolate chips
green M&M's
yellow cake decorating candy sprinkles

What You'll Need

- 30- by 8-inch piece of cardboard • foil • clear tape
- microwave-safe bowl • medium mixing bowl
- 13- by 9- by 2-inch baking pan, ungreased
- wooden spoon • potholders
- medium saucepan • rubber spatula
- utility knife • metal spatula

Directions

1. Cover the cardboard with foil, and secure foil ends to the back of cardboard with clear tape (this will be your serving platter).

2. Preheat oven to 350°. Place 6 tablespoons margarine (or butter) in microwave-safe bowl and heat on high in the microwave until melted. In a medium mixing bowl, combine melted butter or margarine with oats, sugar, flour, nuts, and baking soda, then spread in an ungreased baking pan. Firmly pack with a wooden spoon. Bake crumb crust in the oven for 10 minutes, then remove, using the potholders. Do not turn off the oven.

3. Place 2 tablespoons margarine (or butter) in a saucepan with sweetened condensed milk. Heat and stir with a rubber spatula until it thickens. Turn off burner, stir in 1 teaspoon vanilla, and mix well. Pour warm liquid over crumb crust, then return pan to oven for another 10 to 12 minutes.

4. Remove pan from the oven and immediately sprinkle chocolate chips evenly over the top. As they melt, spread chocolate evenly with a rubber spatula, like frosting.

5. Follow the diagram below to cut cookies with a knife (ask an adult to help you with this). Arrange cookies on cardboard, using a metal spatula, to create a slithering python.

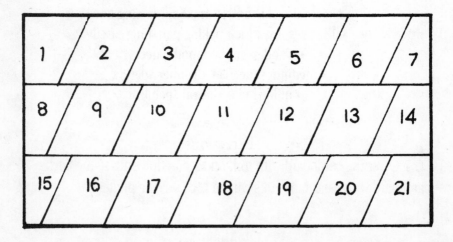

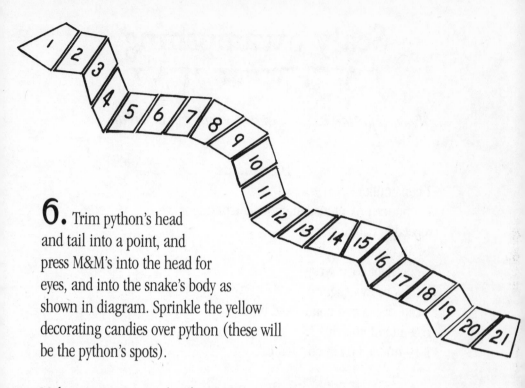

6. Trim python's head and tail into a point, and press M&M's into the head for eyes, and into the snake's body as shown in diagram. Sprinkle the yellow decorating candies over python (these will be the python's spots).

Makes: 1 approximately 24-inch-long people-eating python

Scaly Swampthing

The Swamp Man lives . . . and he wants you for his dinner!

Ingredients

2 cups milk
1 6-ounce box of instant chocolate pudding
vegetable cooking spray
1 cup butter
¾ cup light corn syrup
2 cups brown sugar
1 can sweetened condensed milk
green food coloring
1 19-ounce box of cornflakes

What You'll Need

• small bowl • whisk • 13- by 9- by 2-inch glass pan, ungreased
• wooden spoon • waxed paper • ruler • 4-quart pot • potholders

Directions

1. Pour milk and chocolate pudding into a small bowl. Whisk thoroughly and pour into a glass pan. Chill in refrigerator about 30 minutes, or until set.

2. Spray your wooden spoon liberally with vegetable spray and set aside. Lay a large sheet of waxed paper, about 24 inches, onto your work surface.

3. Place butter, corn syrup, and brown sugar in a pot on the stove. Heat and stir with wooden spoon until mixture begins to bubble. Pour in condensed milk and add food coloring one drop at a time, until you get the shade of swamp green that you want. Bring mixture to a boil and stir for another minute.

4. With an adult's help, take the pot off the stove and pour the cornflakes into the mixture. Use the wooden spoon to mix ingredients together. Allow the mixture to cool just enough to handle.

5. Shape cornflake mix, which will be solid and sticky, into one large Swamp Man figure. Stick him securely in the pudding mixture.

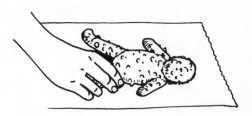

6. When you're ready to serve, encourage each guest to rip off a limb and dip it in the "mud."

Makes: 1 sludge-sucking swampthing

Petrifying Presentation

For a most impressive presentation, double the recipe and make two swampthings fighting each other. Add small dabs of red frosting to show cuts and gashes.

Alien Invader

This horrible head looks disgusting, but its taste is out of this world!

Ingredients
1-pound roll of ready-made cookie dough (any kind)
1 egg white
1 rounded tablespoon liquid glucose
   (available at craft and baking supply stores)
1-pound box of confectioners' sugar (plus an additional ¼ cup)
green food coloring
silver decorating beads
yellow raisins

What You'll Need
• baking sheet • aluminum foil • mixing bowl • kitchen fork
• plastic wrap • utility knife • rolling pin • rubber spatula

Directions

1. Line a baking sheet with foil. Grease and flour the foil lining.

2. To make the special frosting, place egg white, glucose, and 1 cup of confectioners' sugar in a bowl. Add another cup of sugar and several drops of green food coloring. Mix well with a fork, and continue adding confectioners' sugar until icing is very stiff and food coloring is thoroughly blended. If you want your alien darker green, add more food coloring, one drop at a time.

3. Sprinkle a smooth work surface with some extra confectioners' sugar. Knead icing until no longer sticky, then wrap in plastic wrap and set aside.

4. Preheat oven as indicated on the cookie package. With a utility knife, cut the cookie dough roll into four equal parts. Return two portions of the cookie dough to the refrigerator to keep chilled.

5. Place two sections of the dough on the baking sheet and pat them into pear shapes (dough should be at least 1 inch from each other and all sides of the pan). Bake alien heads in oven for 16 to 18 minutes. Remove and allow aliens to cool.

6. Repeat step 5 with the rest of the dough, allowing the pan to cool 10 minutes between batches.

7. Separate icing into four balls. With the rolling pin, roll one of the icing balls to ¼-inch thickness and carefully place on top of an alien head. Press down on the icing with a rubber spatula, molding the icing to the cookie. Then trim off excess icing. At the widest part of the alien head, create eyes and nose with silver decorating beads. Press yellow raisins in as jagged teeth. Repeat with remaining alien heads.

Serves: 4 space invaders

Petrifying Presentation

Plan a UFO scouting expedition in your backyard, and have dessert outside as you search the skies for spaceships.

DEADLY DROP COOKIES

Drop it! The cookie dough, that is. Drop cookies are made by "dropping" balls of cookie batter onto a baking sheet. Follow these tips to make sure yours are "drop-dead" tasty every time:

- Don't overload the spoon—just drop the amount suggested. Too much batter makes for bigger cookies, which can affect your baking time.

- Cool the cookies *exactly* as the recipe indicates.

- Place cookies about 2 inches apart, unless otherwise indicated. This helps them bake evenly and prevents them from "growing" together as they bake.

Fruity Phlegmballs

Ahhhhh-chew! These coughed-up creations will melt in your mouth.

Ingredients
2 cups all-purpose flour
1 teaspoon baking powder
½ teaspoon salt
1½ sticks unsalted butter, softened
¾ cup granulated sugar
1 tablespoon grated lemon rind
½ cup shredded sweet coconut
1 cup shredded raw carrot
6 ounces white-chocolate chips
¼ cup candied cherries or pineapple
3 envelopes unflavored gelatin (such as Knox)

What You'll Need
• small mixing bowl • kitchen fork • electric mixer •
• large mixing bowl • ungreased baking sheet •
• 2-ounce ice-cream scoop • potholders • metal spatula •
• wire rack • microwave-safe cup •

Directions
1. Preheat oven to 375°. Place flour, baking powder, and salt in small mixing bowl and stir together with a fork. Set aside.

2. With an adult's help, use an electric mixer to cream together butter and sugar in large mixing bowl until fluffy. Add lemon rind, coconut, carrots, and—last—flour mixture, until well blended. Then add chips and candied cherries (or candied pineapple).

3. Scoop dough onto an ungreased baking sheet with a 2-ounce ice-cream scoop about 3 inches apart. Use your thumb to press a deep pit into the center of each cookie.

4. Bake cookies in oven for 15 to 20 minutes. Remove from oven with potholders, transfer to wire rack, and allow to cool.

5. To prepare fresh phlegm, empty gelatin into a cup. Follow package's directions for dissolving the gelatin, then place cup in the refrigerator to set. After 20 minutes, stir vigorously with a fork (this will put air bubbles in your phlegm). Return to the fridge until gelatin is the consistency of pudding. Place a large drop of phlegm into the dip in each cookie before putting in the refrigerator for about 15 minutes. Remove cookies from the baking sheet with a metal spatula.

Makes: About 12 bubbly phlegmballs

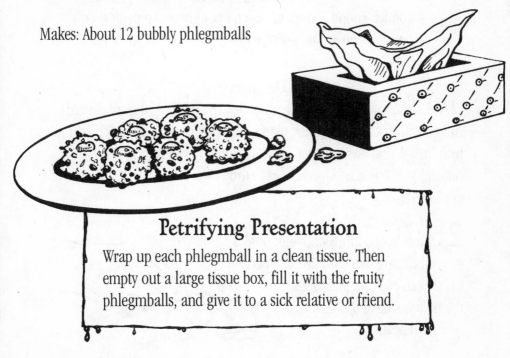

Petrifying Presentation
Wrap up each phlegmball in a clean tissue. Then empty out a large tissue box, fill it with the fruity phlegmballs, and give it to a sick relative or friend.

Brain Bundles

Give your scatterbrained buds something to really think about.

Ingredients
1 cup sweetened condensed milk
2 teaspoons vanilla
1 teaspoon almond extract
¼ teaspoon cinnamon
3 cups sweetened, flaked coconut
1 cup white-chocolate chips
1 cup mini marshmallows
2 to 3 drops black or blue food coloring

What You'll Need
• wooden spoon • large mixing bowl • greased baking sheet
• teaspoon • potholders • wire racks • metal spatula

Directions

1. Preheat oven to 325°. Use a wooden spoon to stir the condensed milk, vanilla, almond extract, cinnamon, coconut, chocolate chips, and mini marshmallows together in a large mixing bowl. To give brains a natural gray color, add food coloring drop by drop until batter is an even shade.

2. Drop teaspoonfuls of dough onto a greased baking sheet, leaving an inch in between each. Lightly press the hollow side of the teaspoon over each brain.

3. Place baking sheet in oven for 13 to 15 minutes (make sure cookies don't burn). With potholders, remove and transfer cookies to wire racks to cool. When cool, use a metal spatula to move cookies to a plate.

Makes: 3 dozen brain transplants

Petrifying Presentation

Brain bundles are a perfect addition to any game night, whether you're shooting hoops in the driveway or playing Trivial Pursuit!

Black-Eyed Ghouls

Some ghouls have all the fun!

Ingredients

2½ cups all-purpose flour
¾ teaspoon cinnamon
½ teaspoon allspice
½ teaspoon ground cloves
½ teaspoon *white* pepper
½ teaspoon baking soda
¼ teaspoon salt
¾ cup raisins
½ cup plus 3 tablespoons
  unsalted butter (not
  margarine), softened

⅔ cup granulated sugar
⅓ cup dark corn syrup
1 large egg
½ cup lemon juice,
  without pulp
1 teaspoon vanilla
2 tablespoons warm water
1¼ cups confectioners' sugar

What You'll Need

• small mixing bowl • kitchen fork • utility knife
• electric mixer • large mixing bowl • tablespoon
• ungreased baking sheet • potholders • wire rack
• metal spatula • 1-inch-wide pastry brush

Directions

1. Preheat oven to 375°. Place flour, cinnamon, allspice, ground cloves, white pepper, baking soda, and salt into a small mixing bowl and stir with a fork, then set aside.

2. Separate raisins into three piles: small, medium, and large. Take the medium-size raisins and, using a utility knife with an adult's help, sliver them in thirds, lengthwise (these slivers will be used later to form the ghoul's mouth).

3. Cream butter and sugar together in a large bowl until smooth. Add corn syrup and egg, and then gradually stir in flour mixture. Blend until dough is stiff. Roll a tablespoon of dough into a ball, then press it lightly to form a disk. Place on an ungreased baking sheet about 2½ inches apart, and repeat with remaining dough.

4. To decorate, place one large and one small raisin on cookie dough as eyes. To give the illusion of a misshapen head, place the right eye slightly higher on the face. Use several medium-size slivers for the mouth.

5. Bake cookies in oven for 13 to 15 minutes until slightly firm. Remove the sheet with potholders and allow to cool on a wire rack. Remove cookies from the sheet with a metal spatula.

6. Whip up a glaze by combining lemon juice, vanilla, water, and confectioners' sugar in a small bowl. Stir well, then use a 1-inch pastry brush to paint each ghoul completely.

Makes: About 18 sweet freaks

Blood Clot Chewies

You'll love the way these cookies bring a lump to your throat.

Ingredients
3 tablespoons margarine
10-ounce package large marshmallows (about 40)
3.4-ounce package cherry-flavored gelatin
6 cups baked rice cereal

What You'll Need
• waxed paper • ruler • vegetable cooking spray (such as Pam)
• large wooden spoon • large microwave-safe bowl
• plastic wrap

Directions

1. Place two 15-inch-long sheets of waxed paper side by side on your work surface. Spray your wooden spoon with vegetable spray.

2. With an adult's help, place margarine and marshmallows in microwave-safe bowl, cover lightly with plastic wrap, and heat on high in the microwave for about 2 minutes. Remove and stir with wooden spoon.

3. Return the covered mixture to the microwave and heat on high for about 1 minute longer (or until marshmallows appear bubbly). Remove, pour in cherry gelatin, and quickly stir until smooth. Add rice cereal and stir gently until well coated.

4. Use your wooden spoon to drop blood clots by spoonfuls onto the waxed paper. (Make your blood clots all different shapes and sizes.) Cool for about 30 minutes.

Makes: About 20 to 30 bloody blobs

Petrifying Presentation

Serve blood clots on cutout paper hearts so everyone can enjoy a heart-attack-sized blood clot to munch on.

Deadly Quicksand Sinkers

Feel bogged down? Sink your teeth into one of these before you go (under!).

Ingredients

2 cups all-purpose flour
½ teaspoon baking powder
¼ teaspoon salt
½ cup butter
½ cup light brown sugar, firmly packed
½ cup granulated sugar
1 large egg
½ cup sour cream
1 teaspoon vanilla extract
1 cup semisweet chocolate chips

What You'll Need

• small mixing bowl • kitchen fork • electric mixer • large mixing bowl • rubber spatula • microwave-safe bowl • wooden spoon • ungreased baking sheet • potholders • wire rack • metal spatula

Directions

1. Preheat oven to 300°. Place flour, baking powder, and salt together in a small mixing bowl and stir with a fork. Set aside.

2. Ask an adult to help you cream together butter and sugars in a large bowl, using an electric mixer. Add egg, sour cream, and vanilla. Gradually stir in flour mixture with a rubber spatula, and continue beating until just combined. Set aside.

3. Place chocolate chips in microwave-safe bowl and microwave on high for about 30 seconds (or until chocolate is melted). Allow chocolate to cool for 3 minutes.

4. Pour warm chocolate over cookie dough (be careful, it could be hot!). Using a wooden spoon, lightly fold chocolate into the dough. The cookie dough should now have the appearance of swirling quicksand with light and dark areas.

5. Drop tablespoonfuls of dough onto ungreased baking sheet about 2 inches apart. Place in the oven for 20 to 25 minutes. Remove with potholders and allow to cool on a wire rack. Transfer cookies to a plate using a metal spatula.

Makes: About 30 deathtraps

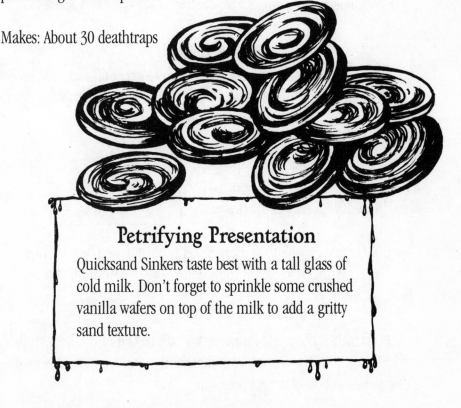

Petrifying Presentation

Quicksand Sinkers taste best with a tall glass of cold milk. Don't forget to sprinkle some crushed vanilla wafers on top of the milk to add a gritty sand texture.

Tasty Traps

If you get stuck in one of these webs, you'd better start preying.

Ingredients
6 ounces yogurt-covered raisins
48 thin pretzel sticks
6 ounces vanilla-flavored decorating chocolate (such as Guittards
    Melt 'N Mold, available at craft and baking supply stores)

What You'll Need
• utility knife • waxed paper • microwave-safe glass measuring cup
• potholders • heavyweight plastic frozen storage bag • scissors

Directions

1. Ask an adult to help you use a utility knife to cut off two short ends of yogurt-covered raisins. This will expose a dark-colored trapped prey inside the spider's "spun cocoon." Set them aside.

2. Arrange eight pretzels on the waxed paper like spokes on a wagon wheel. Repeat with remaining pretzels.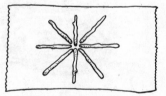

3. Place white chocolate in a microwave-safe cup and heat on high in the microwave until completely melted. Remove cup from microwave with potholders.

4. Pour melted chocolate into a plastic bag (you might ask an adult to help you with this). When bag is cool enough for you to hold, snip off a tiny corner so chocolate can pour out.

5. Squirt a large dot of white chocolate into the center of the pretzels, where they join together. Press one of the yogurt-covered raisins into this dot. Squirt a small circle around the pretzels, connecting them together at their centers. Squirt a large circle around the outer rim of the pretzels to complete the web. Repeat with remaining pretzel circles, then refrigerate until firm.

6. Gently peel webs away from waxed paper and serve.

Serves: 6 people you want to really "bug"

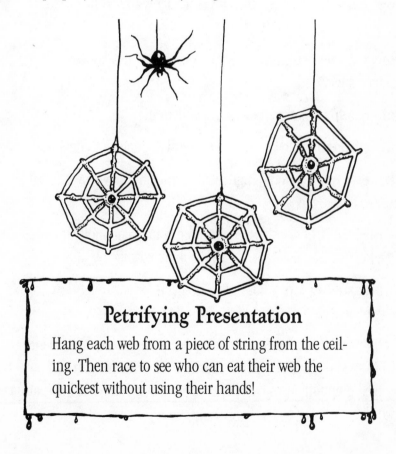

Petrifying Presentation

Hang each web from a piece of string from the ceiling. Then race to see who can eat their web the quickest without using their hands!

Ghastly Glossary

bake - to cook in an oven

beat - to stir quickly with an electric mixer or wire whisk. This adds air and gives the mixture a smoother, fluffier consistency.

blend - to mix ingredients until thoroughly combined

brown sugar - sugar processed with a dark brown syrup that gives it a soft, and slightly sticky, texture

chop - to cut up food into tiny pieces, either with a knife or food processor

confectioners' sugar - finely ground sugar (also known as powdered sugar)

cool - to bring a hot item to room temperature

cutting board - wooden or acrylic board designed for chopping

drizzle - to pour a liquid ingredient evenly and slowly over dough, batter, or baked goods

dry ingredients - any ingredients that contain no moisture, such as sugar, flour, spices, baking soda, and baking powder

dry measuring cup - has a flat, level rim for accurately leveling off dry ingredients

electric mixer - an electric mixing device that mixes ingredients quickly and evenly. If you don't have one, most recipes can also be mixed manually using a wooden spoon, heavy-duty rubber spatula, or whisk.

flour sifter - container with a fine mesh screen at its base that fluffs and removes lumps from flour or other dry ingredients

fold - a gentle way to combine ingredients with *minimal* mixing. It is often used to combine light fluffy ingredients, such as egg whites, with heavier ingredients, such as batter.

granulated sugar - standard white table sugar

grease or **grease and flour pans** - *To grease:* rub butter, margarine, or shortening with a paper towel inside a pan to coat it (this prevents food from sticking during the baking process). *To grease and flour:* sprinkle a small amount of flour over greased interior of pan, coating evenly.

kitchen scissors - scissors used exclusively in the kitchen for food items

knead - to smooth and mix dough by folding it over and over using your hands and knuckles

liquid measuring cup - cup, often made of glass or clear plastic, with a pour spout that measures liquids

pastry bag - Pastry bags can be purchased in most supermarket baking sections or craft supply stores. A heavy-duty plastic bag, snipped at one corner and filled with cookie dough or frosting, also makes a quick and easy pastry bag.

potholder - thick fabric square used to protect hands when handling hot items

preheat - to heat up the oven so that the temperature is correct when you put items in to bake

rolling pin - a round, smooth rod (usually made of wood) used to flatten dough

rubber spatula - spatula with a flat flexible tip, used for scraping bowls and evenly spreading ingredients

separate eggs - to separate the yellow yolk from the egg white. Gently, but firmly, crack the egg against the rim of a bowl. Hold the egg over the clean, dry bowl and carefully rock the yolk back and forth in the shell while allowing the egg white to fall into the bowl. If the yolk breaks open, toss out the egg, or save it for scrambling later.

serrated knife - jagged-edged knife

soften butter or margarine - to bring it to room temperature. Softening times will vary, depending on the weather.

stir - to slowly mix ingredients using a circular motion without adding air to them

utility knife - 6- to 8-inch knife with a smooth, sharp blade

wet ingredients - any ingredients that are liquid or contain moisture, such as eggs, milk, vanilla, butter, and margarine

whisk - a small wire tool used to whip or mix ingredients

wire rack - elevated wire tray used to speed cooling of cookies or other baked goods

wooden spoon - spoon made of wood (often with a long handle), used for stirring and mixing

9- by 13- by 2-inch baking pan - a popular pan dimension commonly required in baking

12- by 15-inch baking sheet - standard-size baking sheet